Blu...
G...
blue gray with
dark forehead

...Warbler
white chin, thin
breast band,
female
duller

Indigo
Bunting
blue with
dark wings

female brown

male

Tree Swallow
white chin
and chest

Eastern Bluebird
sky blue with
rusty chest,
female duller

Barn Swallow
orange forehead,
forked tail,
female duller

Blue Grosbeak
rusty wing bars

female brown

male

female

Purple
Martin
nearly black,
notched tail,
female
gray belly

male

4"   4"   5 1/2"   5 1/2"   7"   7"   7"   8 1/2"

Mostly blue

Blue Jay
blue crest, black necklace

Belted Kingfisher
shaggy crest, female has two bands on chest

Mostly yellow

Blue-winged Warbler

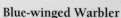

yellow cap, black eye line, dark eyes, female duller

female

Lesser Goldfinch
black cap, female lacks black cap

male

Tennessee Warbler
grayish chin and chest, female less gray

Wilson's Warbler
black cap, female lacks cap

12"   13"   4 1/2"   4 1/2"   4 3/4"   4 3/4"

Mostly yellow

American Goldfinch

female

male

black forehead, female lacks black forehead

American Redstart

yellow patches, white belly

female

male orange

Common Yellowthroat

black mask, female lacks mask

Magnolia Warbler

black necklace, thick streaks on chest, female less black

Orange-crowned Warbler

dull yellow, thin bill

Prairie Warbler

chestnut streaks on back

Worm-eating Warbler

black line through dark eyes, striped head

Yellow Warbler

orange streaks on chest, female lacks streaks

5"   5"   5"   5"   5"   5"   5"   5"

Mostly yellow

Kentucky Warbler

black cap, yellow around eyes

Hooded Warbler

black chin and head patch, female partial patch

Palm Warbler

chestnut cap, yellow eyebrows

Pine Warbler

yellow eye-ring, white wing bars, female duller

Prothonotary Warbler

yellow with gray wings

Dickcissel

female

black bib, female lacks bib

male

Bobolink

pale nape, dark forehead, thin eye line

male black

female

Scarlet Tanager

yellowish with dark wings

male red

female

5"   5 1/4"   5 1/2"   5 1/2"   5 1/2"   6"   7"   7"

Mostly yellow

Yellow-breasted Chat

yellow chin and chest, white around eyes

Baltimore Oriole

pale yellow, white wing bars

male orange

female

Orchard Oriole

dull yellow, white wing bars

male orange

female

female

Evening Grosbeak

bright yellow eyebrows, large ivory bill, female duller

male

Summer Tanager

large bill

male red

female

Eastern Meadowlark

black V on chest, white outer tail feathers as seen in flight

Western Meadowlark

black V on chest, white outer tail feathers as seen in flight

7 1/2"   7 1/2"   7 1/2"   8"   8"   9"   9"

Brown Creeper
long curved bill

House Finch
brown cap, streaked flanks and belly

male red

female

Pine Siskin
yellow streaks on wings, female less yellow

Chipping Sparrow
rusty cap, clear chest

Chimney Swift
pointed head and tail as seen in flight

Chestnut-sided Warbler
yellow cap, chestnut sides, female duller

House Wren
short curved bill

Carolina Wren
white eyebrows, white markings on sides of neck

5"   5"   5"   5"   5"   5"   5"   5 1/2"

Bewick's Wren

white eyebrows, curved bill

Dark-eyed Junco

brown with white belly

male gray

female

Song Sparrow

central dark spot on streaked chest

Cliff Swallow

tan-to-rust forehead and cheeks

Indigo Bunting

brown with lighter throat

male blue

female

Northern Rough-winged Swallow

plain brown with gray belly

Hermit Thrush

dark spots on chest, rusty tail

Louisiana Waterthrush

heavily streaked chest, white eyebrows

5 1/2" 5 1/2" 5 1/2" 5 1/2" 5 1/2" 5 1/2" 6" 6"

Purple Finch
white eye stripe

male red

female

American Tree Sparrow
rusty cap, central dark spot on clear chest

House Sparrow
female

black throat, gray cap, female tan eyebrows

male

Lark Sparrow
bold head pattern, central dark spot on white chest

White-throated Sparrow
white chin, bold eyebrows

White-crowned Sparrow
black and white head

Fox Sparrow
heavily streaked chest and belly

Blue Grosbeak
brown with tan wing bars

male blue

female

6"   6"   6"   6 1/2"   6 1/2"   7"   7"   7"

Brown-headed Cowbird

whitish throat

male black

female

Rose-breasted Grosbeak

bold white eyebrows

male black & white

female

Horned Lark

white-to-yellow throat, black necklace, female duller

Eastern Towhee

rusty sides, red eyes

male black

female

Cedar Waxwing

black mask, red wing tips

Wood Thrush

rusty head, black spots on chest and belly

Red-winged Blackbird

light eyebrows

male black

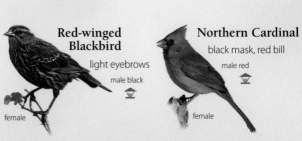

female

Northern Cardinal

black mask, red bill

male red

female

7 1/2"   7 1/2"   7 1/2"   7 1/2"   7 1/2"   8"   8 1/2"   8 1/2"

Mostly brown

Common Nighthawk

white chin, white band across wings as seen in flight, female tan chin

Northern Bobwhite

white eyebrows and chin, female tan eyebrows and chin

Whip-poor-will

large dark eyes, gray on back

Killdeer

two black bands around neck

Brown Thrasher

long tail, long curved bill

Yellow-billed Cuckoo

white chin, dark bars on long tail

Chuck-will's-widow

big head, large dark eyes, small bill

Mourning Dove

blue eye-ring, bobs head while walking

9"   10"   10"   11"   11"   12"   12"   12"

Northern Flicker

yellow wing linings, black mark on face, female lacks black mark

Boat-tailed Grackle

brown head, long tail, dark eyes

female

male black

Greater Prairie-Chicken

yellow skin above eyes, short wide tail

Greater Roadrunner

large bill, long tail

female

Wild Turkey

bare skin on head, black beard, female lacks beard

male

12"   15"   17"   23"   42"

Ruby-throated Hummingbird

ruby throat, female lacks ruby throat

Painted Bunting

female

male

blue head, orange chest, female all green

Green-tailed Towhee

red cap, white throat

Green Jay

blue crown, black face and neck, green body and wings

Monk Parakeet

gray forehead, chin and chest

3 1/4"   5 1/2"   7 1/4"   10 1/2"   12"

Golden-crowned Kinglet

gold and orange on head, female lacks orange

Ruby-crowned Kinglet

white wing bars

Northern Parula

gray head, yellow throat and chest

Brown-headed Nuthatch

brown cap, white cheeks

Red-breasted Nuthatch

black eye line, female gray cap

White-eyed Vireo

yellow on flanks and face, white eyes

Black-capped Chickadee

black cap, white cheeks, white wing edges

Carolina Chickadee

black cap, gray cheeks, gray wing edges

4"   4"   4"   4 1/2"   4 1/2"   5"   5"   5"

Mostly gray

Dark-eyed Junco

white belly, pink bill

female brown

male

White-breasted Nuthatch

black cap, white cheeks, female duller cap

Yellow-rumped Warbler

white chin, bold yellow patches, female duller

Yellow-throated Warbler

yellow chin, black face, female duller

Warbling Vireo

small bill, white eyebrows, dark eyes

Red-eyed Vireo

white eye line, red eyes

Tufted Titmouse

large crest

Black-crested Titmouse

black crest

5 1/2"   5 1/2"   5 1/2"   5 1/2"   5 1/2"   6"   6"   6"

Common Ground-Dove

gray nape, dark-tipped red bill

Eastern Phoebe

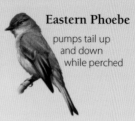

pumps tail up and down while perched

Great Crested Flycatcher

yellow belly, long rusty tail

Eastern Kingbird

white-tipped tail

Gray Catbird

chestnut patch under tail

Loggerhead Shrike

black mask

Northern Mockingbird

long tail, white wing bars

American Robin

black head, female gray head

6 1/2"   7"   8"   8"   9"   9"   10"   10"

Mostly gray

White-winged Dove
blue ring around eyes, white wing edges
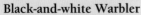

Eurasian Collared-Dove
thin black line on neck

Rock Pigeon
variety of colors

Mostly black & white

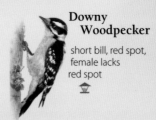

Black-and-white Warbler
black throat and cheeks, female lacks black patches

Downy Woodpecker
short bill, red spot, female lacks red spot

11"   12 1/2"   13"   5"   6"

Red-cockaded Woodpecker

black cap, white face

Rose-breasted Grosbeak

rose chest patch

female brown

male

Yellow-bellied Sapsucker

red cap and chin, female white chin and throat

Hairy Woodpecker

large bill, red spot, female lacks red spot

Red-headed Woodpecker

red head

Red-bellied Woodpecker

red cap and nape, female gray cap

Scissor-tailed Flycatcher

pink wing linings, long tail, female shorter tail

Pileated Woodpecker

red crest and mustache, female black forehead

7"   7 1/2"   8 1/2"   9"   9"   9 1/4"   10"   19"

Mostly black

Bobolink

yellow nape, white shoulders and rump

female yellow

male

Brown-headed Cowbird

brown head, gray bill

male

female brown

European Starling

bill yellow in summer, gray in winter

Eastern Towhee

black head and chest, red eyes

female brown

male

Red-winged Blackbird

red and yellow shoulder patches

female brown

male

Common Grackle

blue head, long tail, female shorter tail

Boat-tailed Grackle

very long tail, yellow eyes

female brown

male

Fish Crow

black with nasal "cah" call

7"   7 1/2"   7 1/2"   7 1/2"   8 1/2"   12"   15"   16"

Mostly black

American Crow
black with familiar "caw" call

Mostly orange

American Redstart
orange patches

female yellow

male

Orchard Oriole
black head, rusty body

female yellow

male

Baltimore Oriole
black head, white wing bars

male

female yellow

18"   5"   7 1/2"   7 1/2"

House Finch

brown cap

female brown

male

Purple Finch

red cap

female brown

male

Scarlet Tanager

black wings and tail

female yellow

male

Summer Tanager

overall red

female yellow

male

Northern Cardinal

black mask, red crest, red bill

male   female brown

5"   6"   7"   8"   8 1/2"

Bluebirds

Favorite: mealworms
Also: dried fruit

Cardinals

Favorite: black oil sunflower seeds
Also: striped sunflower seeds, safflower, millet, cracked corn,
peanut butter

Chickadees, Nuthatches & Titmice

Favorite: black oil sunflower seeds
Also: striped sunflower seeds, safflower, millet, Nyjer thistle,
peanut butter, suet, shelled peanuts, nectar, cracked
corn, mealworms, fruit

Doves

Favorite: millet
Also: cracked corn, safflower, hulled sunflower seeds, milo

Finches (including Grosbeaks)

Favorite: Nyjer thistle
Also: millet, black oil sunflower seeds, striped sunflower seeds,
hulled sunflower seeds, cracked corn, safflower, orange
halves, grape jelly

Hummingbirds

Favorite: nectar

Jays & Crows

Favorite: grape jelly
Also: shelled peanuts, black oil sunflower seeds, peanut butter,
whole or cracked corn, bread crumbs, dried fruit, suet, milo

Orioles

Favorite: grape jelly
Also: orange halves, mealworms, nectar

Sparrows (including Juncos & Towhees)

Favorite: cracked corn
Also: millet, black oil sunflower seeds, striped sunflower
seeds, hulled sunflower seeds, safflower

Woodpeckers (including Flickers & Sapsuckers)

Favorite: suet
Also: shelled peanuts, nuts, acorns, peanut butter, black oil
sunflower seeds, mealworms, dried fruit, orange halves,
whole corn, grape jelly

Adventure Quick Guides

Only Birds of the South
Organized by color
for quick and easy identification

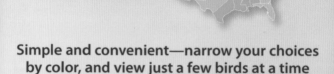

Simple and convenient—narrow your choices by color, and view just a few birds at a time

- Pocket-sized format—easier than laminated foldouts

- Professional photos showing key markings

- Bird feeder icon and feeding guide

- Silhouettes and sizes for quick comparison

- Based on Stan Tekiela's best-selling bird field guides

Improve your birding skills with this beginner's guide that's part how-to book and part field guide.

ISBN 978-1-64755-031-8   U.S. $9.95

5 0 9 9 5

9 781647 550318

NATURE/BIRDS/SOUTH